More Journals!

Want a Journal to give your busy friend or family member as a gift, or just want more Journal ideas?

Check out some of our other Journals...

Your Weekly Self Care Checklist
Gratitude Leaf: Creative Gratitude Journal
Weekly Better Health Checklist
Your Weekly Mental Health Checklist
Your Weekly Happiness Checklist
The Wheel of Life Workbook
The Positivity Workbook
Your Weekly Self Improvement Checklist

Choose from different lengths (60 days, 90 days and more) as well as different types of journals (with different goals and objectives). You are sure to find something that'll be great both as a personal journal and as a gift!

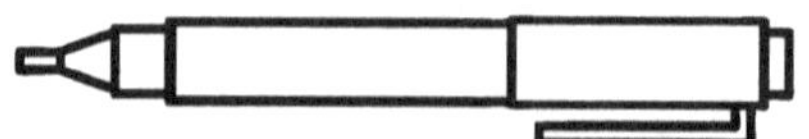

Free Gift!

Want a free gift?

Email us at
betterlifejournals@gmail.com

Title the email "Journal" and we will send you something fun!

Visit our website for more:
https://lifelabmagazine.com/better-life-journals/

YOUR WEEKLY ME-TIME CHECKLIST

DREAM BIG,
WORK HARD,
MAKE IT
happen.

GETTING STARTED

The workbook and journal is pretty self-explanatory so you can just go through it at your own pace. That said, here are some tips that can help you get the most out of this:

- **Schedule a specific time** in the day when you will work on this workbook over the coming days. Having a specific time will help you stay on course. An easy way to do this is to schedule a recurring reminder on your phone's calendar.
- Start with the **Personal Assessment**.
- Next, work on the empowering **habit creator** section. This can help you create one good habit over the next 90 days, which will have a big impact on your wellbeing and happiness.
- Go through the Wellbeing activities list to get ideas for what you can do to take better care of yourself.
- Complete the journal pages every week (ideally daily) over the coming days. Take a bit of time before you get started to mentally prepare yourself if you need to but once you start, commit to doing them every day.

Most importantly, take it one day at a time. Small actions overtime will get you big results, as you will soon find out :)

Let's begin!

Love yourself first, and everything else falls in line. You really have to love yourself to get anything done in this world

PERSONAL ASSESSMENT

1. What does me-time mean to me?

2. What does taking care of myself better look like?

3. Current level of me-time   1 2 3 4 5

4. Desired level of me-time   1 2 3 4 5

PERSONAL ASSESSMENT

5. Why is it important for me to look after myself?

6. Who is the most self-cared person I know, and what do I like most about them/their life?

7. What are the things I can do regularly to look after myself better (both both big and small, like practicing gratitude every day)?

DECLARATION

I hereby commit to this daily practice.

Sign:

Date:

Our bodies are our gardens, to the which our wills are gardeners

WILLIAM SHAKESPEARE

EMPOWERING HABIT CREATOR

Pick one small thing you can do every day for the next 90 days, something that will make you feel good (e.g. gratitude log, meditation, random acts of kindness, etc).

Once you have decided, use the habit tracker below to stick to this small daily positive habit by ticking/coloring one box for every day you practice the habit.

ONE THING = ___________________________

1

30

60

90

It is so important to take time for yourself and find clarity. The most important relationship is the one you have with yourself

DIANE VON FURSTENBERG

WELLBEING ACTIVITIES

Make a list of things that make you feel happy/good (we've included some ideas to get you started). Taking care of yourself is a must when it comes to achieving your goals, as they help you to keep going, and fuels your success.

This list will come in very handy when planning your daily activities, and especially on days you aren't feeling so good (we all have off days, so it's ok).

- ○ Workout (even a 3-5 minutes of physical exercise can have a positive impact on your mood, and wellbeing)

- ○ Practice gratitude (practicing gratitude can not only help you feel good in the short term, but in the long term too!)

- ○ Meditation (practicing meditation can help you to regulate your emotions, and stress, better)

- ○ Random acts of kindness (being nice & helping others is one of the best ways, if not the best way, to feel joy)

- ○ Enjoy a nice cup of your favorite tea or coffee (even small things like this can have a big impact on your mood)

- ○

WELLBEING ACTIVITIES

Don't sacrifice yourself too much, because if you sacrifice too much there's nothing else you can give, and nobody will care for you

KARL LAGERFELD

START YOUR JOURNEY!

DO
YOUR BEST

WEEK OF:

MY PRIORITIES FOR THIS WEEK

GRATITUDE LOG:

MAIN GOALS:

DAILY ACTIVITIES

	M	T	W	T	F	S	S
Daily gratitude log	◯	◯	◯	◯	◯	◯	◯
Do something fun	◯	◯	◯	◯	◯	◯	◯
8 glasses of water	◯	◯	◯	◯	◯	◯	◯
Meditate	◯	◯	◯	◯	◯	◯	◯
Daily journaling	◯	◯	◯	◯	◯	◯	◯
Exercise	◯	◯	◯	◯	◯	◯	◯
Do something important	◯	◯	◯	◯	◯	◯	◯
Do something good	◯	◯	◯	◯	◯	◯	◯
Eat healthy	◯	◯	◯	◯	◯	◯	◯
Read/listen to something good	◯	◯	◯	◯	◯	◯	◯
Connect with others	◯	◯	◯	◯	◯	◯	◯

WEEK OF:

MY PRIORITIES FOR THIS WEEK

GRATITUDE LOG:

MAIN GOALS:

DAILY ACTIVITIES

	M	T	W	T	F	S	S
Daily gratitude log	○	○	○	○	○	○	○
Do something fun	○	○	○	○	○	○	○
8 glasses of water	○	○	○	○	○	○	○
Meditate	○	○	○	○	○	○	○
Daily journaling	○	○	○	○	○	○	○
Exercise	○	○	○	○	○	○	○
Do something important	○	○	○	○	○	○	○
Do something good	○	○	○	○	○	○	○
Eat healthy	○	○	○	○	○	○	○
Read/listen to something good	○	○	○	○	○	○	○
Connect with others	○	○	○	○	○	○	○

MY PRIORITIES FOR THIS WEEK

GRATITUDE LOG:

MAIN GOALS:

DAILY ACTIVITIES

	M	T	W	T	F	S	S
Daily gratitude log	○	○	○	○	○	○	○
Do something fun	○	○	○	○	○	○	○
8 glasses of water	○	○	○	○	○	○	○
Meditate	○	○	○	○	○	○	○
Daily journaling	○	○	○	○	○	○	○
Exercise	○	○	○	○	○	○	○
Do something important	○	○	○	○	○	○	○
Do something good	○	○	○	○	○	○	○
Eat healthy	○	○	○	○	○	○	○
Read/listen to something good	○	○	○	○	○	○	○
Connect with others	○	○	○	○	○	○	○

WEEK OF:

MY PRIORITIES FOR THIS WEEK

GRATITUDE LOG:

MAIN GOALS:

DAILY ACTIVITIES

	M	T	W	T	F	S	S
Daily gratitude log	○	○	○	○	○	○	○
Do something fun	○	○	○	○	○	○	○
8 glasses of water	○	○	○	○	○	○	○
Meditate	○	○	○	○	○	○	○
Daily journaling	○	○	○	○	○	○	○
Exercise	○	○	○	○	○	○	○
Do something important	○	○	○	○	○	○	○
Do something good	○	○	○	○	○	○	○
Eat healthy	○	○	○	○	○	○	○
Read/listen to something good	○	○	○	○	○	○	○
Connect with others	○	○	○	○	○	○	○

WEEK OF:

MY PRIORITIES FOR THIS WEEK

GRATITUDE LOG:

MAIN GOALS:

DAILY ACTIVITIES

	M	T	W	T	F	S	S
Daily gratitude log	◯	◯	◯	◯	◯	◯	◯
Do something fun	◯	◯	◯	◯	◯	◯	◯
8 glasses of water	◯	◯	◯	◯	◯	◯	◯
Meditate	◯	◯	◯	◯	◯	◯	◯
Daily journaling	◯	◯	◯	◯	◯	◯	◯
Exercise	◯	◯	◯	◯	◯	◯	◯
Do something important	◯	◯	◯	◯	◯	◯	◯
Do something good	◯	◯	◯	◯	◯	◯	◯
Eat healthy	◯	◯	◯	◯	◯	◯	◯
Read/listen to something good	◯	◯	◯	◯	◯	◯	◯
Connect with others	◯	◯	◯	◯	◯	◯	◯

WEEK OF:

MY PRIORITIES FOR THIS WEEK

GRATITUDE LOG:

MAIN GOALS:

DAILY ACTIVITIES

	M	T	W	T	F	S	S
Daily gratitude log	○	○	○	○	○	○	○
Do something fun	○	○	○	○	○	○	○
8 glasses of water	○	○	○	○	○	○	○
Meditate	○	○	○	○	○	○	○
Daily journaling	○	○	○	○	○	○	○
Exercise	○	○	○	○	○	○	○
Do something important	○	○	○	○	○	○	○
Do something good	○	○	○	○	○	○	○
Eat healthy	○	○	○	○	○	○	○
Read/listen to something good	○	○	○	○	○	○	○
Connect with others	○	○	○	○	○	○	○

WEEK OF:

MY PRIORITIES FOR THIS WEEK

GRATITUDE LOG:

MAIN GOALS:

DAILY ACTIVITIES

	M	T	W	T	F	S	S
Daily gratitude log	○	○	○	○	○	○	○
Do something fun	○	○	○	○	○	○	○
8 glasses of water	○	○	○	○	○	○	○
Meditate	○	○	○	○	○	○	○
Daily journaling	○	○	○	○	○	○	○
Exercise	○	○	○	○	○	○	○
Do something important	○	○	○	○	○	○	○
Do something good	○	○	○	○	○	○	○
Eat healthy	○	○	○	○	○	○	○
Read/listen to something good	○	○	○	○	○	○	○
Connect with others	○	○	○	○	○	○	○

WEEK OF:

MY PRIORITIES FOR THIS WEEK

GRATITUDE LOG:

MAIN GOALS:

DAILY ACTIVITIES

	M	T	W	T	F	S	S
Daily gratitude log	○	○	○	○	○	○	○
Do something fun	○	○	○	○	○	○	○
8 glasses of water	○	○	○	○	○	○	○
Meditate	○	○	○	○	○	○	○
Daily journaling	○	○	○	○	○	○	○
Exercise	○	○	○	○	○	○	○
Do something important	○	○	○	○	○	○	○
Do something good	○	○	○	○	○	○	○
Eat healthy	○	○	○	○	○	○	○
Read/listen to something good	○	○	○	○	○	○	○
Connect with others	○	○	○	○	○	○	○

WEEK OF:

MY PRIORITIES FOR THIS WEEK

GRATITUDE LOG:

MAIN GOALS:

DAILY ACTIVITIES

	M	T	W	T	F	S	S
Daily gratitude log	○	○	○	○	○	○	○
Do something fun	○	○	○	○	○	○	○
8 glasses of water	○	○	○	○	○	○	○
Meditate	○	○	○	○	○	○	○
Daily journaling	○	○	○	○	○	○	○
Exercise	○	○	○	○	○	○	○
Do something important	○	○	○	○	○	○	○
Do something good	○	○	○	○	○	○	○
Eat healthy	○	○	○	○	○	○	○
Read/listen to something good	○	○	○	○	○	○	○
Connect with others	○	○	○	○	○	○	○

WEEK OF:

MY PRIORITIES FOR THIS WEEK

GRATITUDE LOG:

MAIN GOALS:

DAILY ACTIVITIES

	M	T	W	T	F	S	S
Daily gratitude log	○	○	○	○	○	○	○
Do something fun	○	○	○	○	○	○	○
8 glasses of water	○	○	○	○	○	○	○
Meditate	○	○	○	○	○	○	○
Daily journaling	○	○	○	○	○	○	○
Exercise	○	○	○	○	○	○	○
Do something important	○	○	○	○	○	○	○
Do something good	○	○	○	○	○	○	○
Eat healthy	○	○	○	○	○	○	○
Read/listen to something good	○	○	○	○	○	○	○
Connect with others	○	○	○	○	○	○	○

WEEK OF:

MY PRIORITIES FOR THIS WEEK

GRATITUDE LOG:

MAIN GOALS:

DAILY ACTIVITIES

	M	T	W	T	F	S	S
Daily gratitude log	○	○	○	○	○	○	○
Do something fun	○	○	○	○	○	○	○
8 glasses of water	○	○	○	○	○	○	○
Meditate	○	○	○	○	○	○	○
Daily journaling	○	○	○	○	○	○	○
Exercise	○	○	○	○	○	○	○
Do something important	○	○	○	○	○	○	○
Do something good	○	○	○	○	○	○	○
Eat healthy	○	○	○	○	○	○	○
Read/listen to something good	○	○	○	○	○	○	○
Connect with others	○	○	○	○	○	○	○

WEEK OF:

MY PRIORITIES FOR THIS WEEK

GRATITUDE LOG:

MAIN GOALS:

DAILY ACTIVITIES

	M	T	W	T	F	S	S
Daily gratitude log	○	○	○	○	○	○	○
Do something fun	○	○	○	○	○	○	○
8 glasses of water	○	○	○	○	○	○	○
Meditate	○	○	○	○	○	○	○
Daily journaling	○	○	○	○	○	○	○
Exercise	○	○	○	○	○	○	○
Do something important	○	○	○	○	○	○	○
Do something good	○	○	○	○	○	○	○
Eat healthy	○	○	○	○	○	○	○
Read/listen to something good	○	○	○	○	○	○	○
Connect with others	○	○	○	○	○	○	○

WEEK OF:

MY PRIORITIES FOR THIS WEEK

GRATITUDE LOG:

MAIN GOALS:

DAILY ACTIVITIES

	M	T	W	T	F	S	S
Daily gratitude log	○	○	○	○	○	○	○
Do something fun	○	○	○	○	○	○	○
8 glasses of water	○	○	○	○	○	○	○
Meditate	○	○	○	○	○	○	○
Daily journaling	○	○	○	○	○	○	○
Exercise	○	○	○	○	○	○	○
Do something important	○	○	○	○	○	○	○
Do something good	○	○	○	○	○	○	○
Eat healthy	○	○	○	○	○	○	○
Read/listen to something good	○	○	○	○	○	○	○
Connect with others	○	○	○	○	○	○	○

MY PRIORITIES FOR THIS WEEK

GRATITUDE LOG:

MAIN GOALS:

DAILY ACTIVITIES

	M	T	W	T	F	S	S
Daily gratitude log	○	○	○	○	○	○	○
Do something fun	○	○	○	○	○	○	○
8 glasses of water	○	○	○	○	○	○	○
Meditate	○	○	○	○	○	○	○
Daily journaling	○	○	○	○	○	○	○
Exercise	○	○	○	○	○	○	○
Do something important	○	○	○	○	○	○	○
Do something good	○	○	○	○	○	○	○
Eat healthy	○	○	○	○	○	○	○
Read/listen to something good	○	○	○	○	○	○	○
Connect with others	○	○	○	○	○	○	○

WEEK OF:

MY PRIORITIES FOR THIS WEEK

GRATITUDE LOG:

MAIN GOALS:

DAILY ACTIVITIES

	M	T	W	T	F	S	S
Daily gratitude log	○	○	○	○	○	○	○
Do something fun	○	○	○	○	○	○	○
8 glasses of water	○	○	○	○	○	○	○
Meditate	○	○	○	○	○	○	○
Daily journaling	○	○	○	○	○	○	○
Exercise	○	○	○	○	○	○	○
Do something important	○	○	○	○	○	○	○
Do something good	○	○	○	○	○	○	○
Eat healthy	○	○	○	○	○	○	○
Read/listen to something good	○	○	○	○	○	○	○
Connect with others	○	○	○	○	○	○	○

WEEK OF:

MY PRIORITIES FOR THIS WEEK

GRATITUDE LOG:

MAIN GOALS:

DAILY ACTIVITIES

	M	T	W	T	F	S	S
Daily gratitude log	○	○	○	○	○	○	○
Do something fun	○	○	○	○	○	○	○
8 glasses of water	○	○	○	○	○	○	○
Meditate	○	○	○	○	○	○	○
Daily journaling	○	○	○	○	○	○	○
Exercise	○	○	○	○	○	○	○
Do something important	○	○	○	○	○	○	○
Do something good	○	○	○	○	○	○	○
Eat healthy	○	○	○	○	○	○	○
Read/listen to something good	○	○	○	○	○	○	○
Connect with others	○	○	○	○	○	○	○

WEEK OF:

MY PRIORITIES FOR THIS WEEK

GRATITUDE LOG:

MAIN GOALS:

DAILY ACTIVITIES

	M	T	W	T	F	S	S
Daily gratitude log	○	○	○	○	○	○	○
Do something fun	○	○	○	○	○	○	○
8 glasses of water	○	○	○	○	○	○	○
Meditate	○	○	○	○	○	○	○
Daily journaling	○	○	○	○	○	○	○
Exercise	○	○	○	○	○	○	○
Do something important	○	○	○	○	○	○	○
Do something good	○	○	○	○	○	○	○
Eat healthy	○	○	○	○	○	○	○
Read/listen to something good	○	○	○	○	○	○	○
Connect with others	○	○	○	○	○	○	○

WEEK OF:

MY PRIORITIES FOR THIS WEEK

GRATITUDE LOG:

MAIN GOALS:

DAILY ACTIVITIES

	M	T	W	T	F	S	S
Daily gratitude log	○	○	○	○	○	○	○
Do something fun	○	○	○	○	○	○	○
8 glasses of water	○	○	○	○	○	○	○
Meditate	○	○	○	○	○	○	○
Daily journaling	○	○	○	○	○	○	○
Exercise	○	○	○	○	○	○	○
Do something important	○	○	○	○	○	○	○
Do something good	○	○	○	○	○	○	○
Eat healthy	○	○	○	○	○	○	○
Read/listen to something good	○	○	○	○	○	○	○
Connect with others	○	○	○	○	○	○	○

WEEK OF:

MY PRIORITIES FOR THIS WEEK

GRATITUDE LOG:

MAIN GOALS:

DAILY ACTIVITIES

	M	T	W	T	F	S	S
Daily gratitude log	◯	◯	◯	◯	◯	◯	◯
Do something fun	◯	◯	◯	◯	◯	◯	◯
8 glasses of water	◯	◯	◯	◯	◯	◯	◯
Meditate	◯	◯	◯	◯	◯	◯	◯
Daily journaling	◯	◯	◯	◯	◯	◯	◯
Exercise	◯	◯	◯	◯	◯	◯	◯
Do something important	◯	◯	◯	◯	◯	◯	◯
Do something good	◯	◯	◯	◯	◯	◯	◯
Eat healthy	◯	◯	◯	◯	◯	◯	◯
Read/listen to something good	◯	◯	◯	◯	◯	◯	◯
Connect with others	◯	◯	◯	◯	◯	◯	◯

WEEK OF:

MY PRIORITIES FOR THIS WEEK

GRATITUDE LOG:

MAIN GOALS:

DAILY ACTIVITIES

	M	T	W	T	F	S	S
Daily gratitude log	○	○	○	○	○	○	○
Do something fun	○	○	○	○	○	○	○
8 glasses of water	○	○	○	○	○	○	○
Meditate	○	○	○	○	○	○	○
Daily journaling	○	○	○	○	○	○	○
Exercise	○	○	○	○	○	○	○
Do something important	○	○	○	○	○	○	○
Do something good	○	○	○	○	○	○	○
Eat healthy	○	○	○	○	○	○	○
Read/listen to something good	○	○	○	○	○	○	○
Connect with others	○	○	○	○	○	○	○

WEEK OF:

MY PRIORITIES FOR THIS WEEK

GRATITUDE LOG:

MAIN GOALS:

DAILY ACTIVITIES

	M	T	W	T	F	S	S
Daily gratitude log	○	○	○	○	○	○	○
Do something fun	○	○	○	○	○	○	○
8 glasses of water	○	○	○	○	○	○	○
Meditate	○	○	○	○	○	○	○
Daily journaling	○	○	○	○	○	○	○
Exercise	○	○	○	○	○	○	○
Do something important	○	○	○	○	○	○	○
Do something good	○	○	○	○	○	○	○
Eat healthy	○	○	○	○	○	○	○
Read/listen to something good	○	○	○	○	○	○	○
Connect with others	○	○	○	○	○	○	○

WEEK OF:

MY PRIORITIES FOR THIS WEEK

GRATITUDE LOG:

MAIN GOALS:

DAILY ACTIVITIES

	M	T	W	T	F	S	S
Daily gratitude log	○	○	○	○	○	○	○
Do something fun	○	○	○	○	○	○	○
8 glasses of water	○	○	○	○	○	○	○
Meditate	○	○	○	○	○	○	○
Daily journaling	○	○	○	○	○	○	○
Exercise	○	○	○	○	○	○	○
Do something important	○	○	○	○	○	○	○
Do something good	○	○	○	○	○	○	○
Eat healthy	○	○	○	○	○	○	○
Read/listen to something good	○	○	○	○	○	○	○
Connect with others	○	○	○	○	○	○	○

WEEK OF:

MY PRIORITIES FOR THIS WEEK

GRATITUDE LOG:

MAIN GOALS:

DAILY ACTIVITIES

M T W T F S S

Daily gratitude log
Do something fun
8 glasses of water
Meditate
Daily journaling
Exercise
Do something
important
Do something good
Eat healthy
Read/listen
to something good
Connect with others

WEEK OF:

MY PRIORITIES FOR THIS WEEK

GRATITUDE LOG:

MAIN GOALS:

DAILY ACTIVITIES

	M	T	W	T	F	S	S
Daily gratitude log	◯	◯	◯	◯	◯	◯	◯
Do something fun	◯	◯	◯	◯	◯	◯	◯
8 glasses of water	◯	◯	◯	◯	◯	◯	◯
Meditate	◯	◯	◯	◯	◯	◯	◯
Daily journaling	◯	◯	◯	◯	◯	◯	◯
Exercise	◯	◯	◯	◯	◯	◯	◯
Do something important	◯	◯	◯	◯	◯	◯	◯
Do something good	◯	◯	◯	◯	◯	◯	◯
Eat healthy	◯	◯	◯	◯	◯	◯	◯
Read/listen to something good	◯	◯	◯	◯	◯	◯	◯
Connect with others	◯	◯	◯	◯	◯	◯	◯

WEEK OF:

MY PRIORITIES FOR THIS WEEK

GRATITUDE LOG:

MAIN GOALS:

DAILY ACTIVITIES

	M	T	W	T	F	S	S
Daily gratitude log	○	○	○	○	○	○	○
Do something fun	○	○	○	○	○	○	○
8 glasses of water	○	○	○	○	○	○	○
Meditate	○	○	○	○	○	○	○
Daily journaling	○	○	○	○	○	○	○
Exercise	○	○	○	○	○	○	○
Do something important	○	○	○	○	○	○	○
Do something good	○	○	○	○	○	○	○
Eat healthy	○	○	○	○	○	○	○
Read/listen to something good	○	○	○	○	○	○	○
Connect with others	○	○	○	○	○	○	○

WEEK OF:

MY PRIORITIES FOR THIS WEEK

GRATITUDE LOG:

MAIN GOALS:

DAILY ACTIVITIES

	M	T	W	T	F	S	S
Daily gratitude log	○	○	○	○	○	○	○
Do something fun	○	○	○	○	○	○	○
8 glasses of water	○	○	○	○	○	○	○
Meditate	○	○	○	○	○	○	○
Daily journaling	○	○	○	○	○	○	○
Exercise	○	○	○	○	○	○	○
Do something important	○	○	○	○	○	○	○
Do something good	○	○	○	○	○	○	○
Eat healthy	○	○	○	○	○	○	○
Read/listen to something good	○	○	○	○	○	○	○
Connect with others	○	○	○	○	○	○	○

WEEK OF:

MY PRIORITIES FOR THIS WEEK

GRATITUDE LOG:

MAIN GOALS:

DAILY ACTIVITIES

	M	T	W	T	F	S	S
Daily gratitude log	◯	◯	◯	◯	◯	◯	◯
Do something fun	◯	◯	◯	◯	◯	◯	◯
8 glasses of water	◯	◯	◯	◯	◯	◯	◯
Meditate	◯	◯	◯	◯	◯	◯	◯
Daily journaling	◯	◯	◯	◯	◯	◯	◯
Exercise	◯	◯	◯	◯	◯	◯	◯
Do something important	◯	◯	◯	◯	◯	◯	◯
Do something good	◯	◯	◯	◯	◯	◯	◯
Eat healthy	◯	◯	◯	◯	◯	◯	◯
Read/listen to something good	◯	◯	◯	◯	◯	◯	◯
Connect with others	◯	◯	◯	◯	◯	◯	◯

WEEK OF:

MY PRIORITIES FOR THIS WEEK

GRATITUDE LOG: ## MAIN GOALS:

DAILY ACTIVITIES

	M	T	W	T	F	S	S
Daily gratitude log	○	○	○	○	○	○	○
Do something fun	○	○	○	○	○	○	○
8 glasses of water	○	○	○	○	○	○	○
Meditate	○	○	○	○	○	○	○
Daily journaling	○	○	○	○	○	○	○
Exercise	○	○	○	○	○	○	○
Do something important	○	○	○	○	○	○	○
Do something good	○	○	○	○	○	○	○
Eat healthy	○	○	○	○	○	○	○
Read/listen to something good	○	○	○	○	○	○	○
Connect with others	○	○	○	○	○	○	○

WEEK OF:

MY PRIORITIES FOR THIS WEEK

GRATITUDE LOG:

MAIN GOALS:

DAILY ACTIVITIES

	M	T	W	T	F	S	S
Daily gratitude log	○	○	○	○	○	○	○
Do something fun	○	○	○	○	○	○	○
8 glasses of water	○	○	○	○	○	○	○
Meditate	○	○	○	○	○	○	○
Daily journaling	○	○	○	○	○	○	○
Exercise	○	○	○	○	○	○	○
Do something important	○	○	○	○	○	○	○
Do something good	○	○	○	○	○	○	○
Eat healthy	○	○	○	○	○	○	○
Read/listen to something good	○	○	○	○	○	○	○
Connect with others	○	○	○	○	○	○	○

WEEK OF:

MY PRIORITIES FOR THIS WEEK

GRATITUDE LOG:

MAIN GOALS:

DAILY ACTIVITIES

	M	T	W	T	F	S	S
Daily gratitude log	○	○	○	○	○	○	○
Do something fun	○	○	○	○	○	○	○
8 glasses of water	○	○	○	○	○	○	○
Meditate	○	○	○	○	○	○	○
Daily journaling	○	○	○	○	○	○	○
Exercise	○	○	○	○	○	○	○
Do something important	○	○	○	○	○	○	○
Do something good	○	○	○	○	○	○	○
Eat healthy	○	○	○	○	○	○	○
Read/listen to something good	○	○	○	○	○	○	○
Connect with others	○	○	○	○	○	○	○

WEEK OF:

MY PRIORITIES FOR THIS WEEK

GRATITUDE LOG:

MAIN GOALS:

DAILY ACTIVITIES

	M	T	W	T	F	S	S
Daily gratitude log	○	○	○	○	○	○	○
Do something fun	○	○	○	○	○	○	○
8 glasses of water	○	○	○	○	○	○	○
Meditate	○	○	○	○	○	○	○
Daily journaling	○	○	○	○	○	○	○
Exercise	○	○	○	○	○	○	○
Do something important	○	○	○	○	○	○	○
Do something good	○	○	○	○	○	○	○
Eat healthy	○	○	○	○	○	○	○
Read/listen to something good	○	○	○	○	○	○	○
Connect with others	○	○	○	○	○	○	○

WEEK OF:

MY PRIORITIES FOR THIS WEEK

GRATITUDE LOG:

MAIN GOALS:

DAILY ACTIVITIES

	M	T	W	T	F	S	S
Daily gratitude log	○	○	○	○	○	○	○
Do something fun	○	○	○	○	○	○	○
8 glasses of water	○	○	○	○	○	○	○
Meditate	○	○	○	○	○	○	○
Daily journaling	○	○	○	○	○	○	○
Exercise	○	○	○	○	○	○	○
Do something important	○	○	○	○	○	○	○
Do something good	○	○	○	○	○	○	○
Eat healthy	○	○	○	○	○	○	○
Read/listen to something good	○	○	○	○	○	○	○
Connect with others	○	○	○	○	○	○	○

WEEK OF:

MY PRIORITIES FOR THIS WEEK

GRATITUDE LOG:

MAIN GOALS:

DAILY ACTIVITIES

	M	T	W	T	F	S	S
Daily gratitude log	○	○	○	○	○	○	○
Do something fun	○	○	○	○	○	○	○
8 glasses of water	○	○	○	○	○	○	○
Meditate	○	○	○	○	○	○	○
Daily journaling	○	○	○	○	○	○	○
Exercise	○	○	○	○	○	○	○
Do something important	○	○	○	○	○	○	○
Do something good	○	○	○	○	○	○	○
Eat healthy	○	○	○	○	○	○	○
Read/listen to something good	○	○	○	○	○	○	○
Connect with others	○	○	○	○	○	○	○

WEEK OF:

MY PRIORITIES FOR THIS WEEK

GRATITUDE LOG:

MAIN GOALS:

DAILY ACTIVITIES

	M	T	W	T	F	S	S
Daily gratitude log	○	○	○	○	○	○	○
Do something fun	○	○	○	○	○	○	○
8 glasses of water	○	○	○	○	○	○	○
Meditate	○	○	○	○	○	○	○
Daily journaling	○	○	○	○	○	○	○
Exercise	○	○	○	○	○	○	○
Do something important	○	○	○	○	○	○	○
Do something good	○	○	○	○	○	○	○
Eat healthy	○	○	○	○	○	○	○
Read/listen to something good	○	○	○	○	○	○	○
Connect with others	○	○	○	○	○	○	○

WEEK OF:

MY PRIORITIES FOR THIS WEEK

GRATITUDE LOG:

MAIN GOALS:

DAILY ACTIVITIES

	M	T	W	T	F	S	S
Daily gratitude log	○	○	○	○	○	○	○
Do something fun	○	○	○	○	○	○	○
8 glasses of water	○	○	○	○	○	○	○
Meditate	○	○	○	○	○	○	○
Daily journaling	○	○	○	○	○	○	○
Exercise	○	○	○	○	○	○	○
Do something important	○	○	○	○	○	○	○
Do something good	○	○	○	○	○	○	○
Eat healthy	○	○	○	○	○	○	○
Read/listen to something good	○	○	○	○	○	○	○
Connect with others	○	○	○	○	○	○	○

WEEK OF:

MY PRIORITIES FOR THIS WEEK

GRATITUDE LOG:

MAIN GOALS:

DAILY ACTIVITIES

	M	T	W	T	F	S	S
Daily gratitude log	○	○	○	○	○	○	○
Do something fun	○	○	○	○	○	○	○
8 glasses of water	○	○	○	○	○	○	○
Meditate	○	○	○	○	○	○	○
Daily journaling	○	○	○	○	○	○	○
Exercise	○	○	○	○	○	○	○
Do something important	○	○	○	○	○	○	○
Do something good	○	○	○	○	○	○	○
Eat healthy	○	○	○	○	○	○	○
Read/listen to something good	○	○	○	○	○	○	○
Connect with others	○	○	○	○	○	○	○

WEEK OF:

MY PRIORITIES FOR THIS WEEK

GRATITUDE LOG:

MAIN GOALS:

DAILY ACTIVITIES

	M	T	W	T	F	S	S
Daily gratitude log	○	○	○	○	○	○	○
Do something fun	○	○	○	○	○	○	○
8 glasses of water	○	○	○	○	○	○	○
Meditate	○	○	○	○	○	○	○
Daily journaling	○	○	○	○	○	○	○
Exercise	○	○	○	○	○	○	○
Do something important	○	○	○	○	○	○	○
Do something good	○	○	○	○	○	○	○
Eat healthy	○	○	○	○	○	○	○
Read/listen to something good	○	○	○	○	○	○	○
Connect with others	○	○	○	○	○	○	○

WEEK OF:

MY PRIORITIES FOR THIS WEEK

GRATITUDE LOG: MAIN GOALS:

DAILY ACTIVITIES

	M	T	W	T	F	S	S
Daily gratitude log	○	○	○	○	○	○	○
Do something fun	○	○	○	○	○	○	○
8 glasses of water	○	○	○	○	○	○	○
Meditate	○	○	○	○	○	○	○
Daily journaling	○	○	○	○	○	○	○
Exercise	○	○	○	○	○	○	○
Do something important	○	○	○	○	○	○	○
Do something good	○	○	○	○	○	○	○
Eat healthy	○	○	○	○	○	○	○
Read/listen to something good	○	○	○	○	○	○	○
Connect with others	○	○	○	○	○	○	○

WEEK OF:

MY PRIORITIES FOR THIS WEEK

GRATITUDE LOG:

MAIN GOALS:

DAILY ACTIVITIES

	M	T	W	T	F	S	S
Daily gratitude log	○	○	○	○	○	○	○
Do something fun	○	○	○	○	○	○	○
8 glasses of water	○	○	○	○	○	○	○
Meditate	○	○	○	○	○	○	○
Daily journaling	○	○	○	○	○	○	○
Exercise	○	○	○	○	○	○	○
Do something important	○	○	○	○	○	○	○
Do something good	○	○	○	○	○	○	○
Eat healthy	○	○	○	○	○	○	○
Read/listen to something good	○	○	○	○	○	○	○
Connect with others	○	○	○	○	○	○	○

WEEK OF:

MY PRIORITIES FOR THIS WEEK

GRATITUDE LOG:

MAIN GOALS:

DAILY ACTIVITIES

	M	T	W	T	F	S	S
Daily gratitude log	○	○	○	○	○	○	○
Do something fun	○	○	○	○	○	○	○
8 glasses of water	○	○	○	○	○	○	○
Meditate	○	○	○	○	○	○	○
Daily journaling	○	○	○	○	○	○	○
Exercise	○	○	○	○	○	○	○
Do something important	○	○	○	○	○	○	○
Do something good	○	○	○	○	○	○	○
Eat healthy	○	○	○	○	○	○	○
Read/listen to something good	○	○	○	○	○	○	○
Connect with others	○	○	○	○	○	○	○

MY PRIORITIES FOR THIS WEEK

GRATITUDE LOG:

MAIN GOALS:

DAILY ACTIVITIES

	M	T	W	T	F	S	S
Daily gratitude log	○	○	○	○	○	○	○
Do something fun	○	○	○	○	○	○	○
8 glasses of water	○	○	○	○	○	○	○
Meditate	○	○	○	○	○	○	○
Daily journaling	○	○	○	○	○	○	○
Exercise	○	○	○	○	○	○	○
Do something important	○	○	○	○	○	○	○
Do something good	○	○	○	○	○	○	○
Eat healthy	○	○	○	○	○	○	○
Read/listen to something good	○	○	○	○	○	○	○
Connect with others	○	○	○	○	○	○	○

WEEK OF:

MY PRIORITIES FOR THIS WEEK

GRATITUDE LOG:

MAIN GOALS:

DAILY ACTIVITIES

	M	T	W	T	F	S	S
Daily gratitude log	○	○	○	○	○	○	○
Do something fun	○	○	○	○	○	○	○
8 glasses of water	○	○	○	○	○	○	○
Meditate	○	○	○	○	○	○	○
Daily journaling	○	○	○	○	○	○	○
Exercise	○	○	○	○	○	○	○
Do something important	○	○	○	○	○	○	○
Do something good	○	○	○	○	○	○	○
Eat healthy	○	○	○	○	○	○	○
Read/listen to something good	○	○	○	○	○	○	○
Connect with others	○	○	○	○	○	○	○

WEEK OF:

MY PRIORITIES FOR THIS WEEK

GRATITUDE LOG:

MAIN GOALS:

DAILY ACTIVITIES

	M	T	W	T	F	S	S
Daily gratitude log	○	○	○	○	○	○	○
Do something fun	○	○	○	○	○	○	○
8 glasses of water	○	○	○	○	○	○	○
Meditate	○	○	○	○	○	○	○
Daily journaling	○	○	○	○	○	○	○
Exercise	○	○	○	○	○	○	○
Do something important	○	○	○	○	○	○	○
Do something good	○	○	○	○	○	○	○
Eat healthy	○	○	○	○	○	○	○
Read/listen to something good	○	○	○	○	○	○	○
Connect with others	○	○	○	○	○	○	○

WEEK OF:

MY PRIORITIES FOR THIS WEEK

GRATITUDE LOG:

MAIN GOALS:

DAILY ACTIVITIES

	M	T	W	T	F	S	S
Daily gratitude log	○	○	○	○	○	○	○
Do something fun	○	○	○	○	○	○	○
8 glasses of water	○	○	○	○	○	○	○
Meditate	○	○	○	○	○	○	○
Daily journaling	○	○	○	○	○	○	○
Exercise	○	○	○	○	○	○	○
Do something important	○	○	○	○	○	○	○
Do something good	○	○	○	○	○	○	○
Eat healthy	○	○	○	○	○	○	○
Read/listen to something good	○	○	○	○	○	○	○
Connect with others	○	○	○	○	○	○	○

WEEK OF:

MY PRIORITIES FOR THIS WEEK

GRATITUDE LOG:

MAIN GOALS:

DAILY ACTIVITIES

	M	T	W	T	F	S	S
Daily gratitude log	○	○	○	○	○	○	○
Do something fun	○	○	○	○	○	○	○
8 glasses of water	○	○	○	○	○	○	○
Meditate	○	○	○	○	○	○	○
Daily journaling	○	○	○	○	○	○	○
Exercise	○	○	○	○	○	○	○
Do something important	○	○	○	○	○	○	○
Do something good	○	○	○	○	○	○	○
Eat healthy	○	○	○	○	○	○	○
Read/listen to something good	○	○	○	○	○	○	○
Connect with others	○	○	○	○	○	○	○

WEEK OF:

MY PRIORITIES FOR THIS WEEK

GRATITUDE LOG:

MAIN GOALS:

DAILY ACTIVITIES

	M	T	W	T	F	S	S
Daily gratitude log	○	○	○	○	○	○	○
Do something fun	○	○	○	○	○	○	○
8 glasses of water	○	○	○	○	○	○	○
Meditate	○	○	○	○	○	○	○
Daily journaling	○	○	○	○	○	○	○
Exercise	○	○	○	○	○	○	○
Do something important	○	○	○	○	○	○	○
Do something good	○	○	○	○	○	○	○
Eat healthy	○	○	○	○	○	○	○
Read/listen to something good	○	○	○	○	○	○	○
Connect with others	○	○	○	○	○	○	○

MY PRIORITIES FOR THIS WEEK

GRATITUDE LOG:

MAIN GOALS:

DAILY ACTIVITIES

	M	T	W	T	F	S	S
Daily gratitude log	○	○	○	○	○	○	○
Do something fun	○	○	○	○	○	○	○
8 glasses of water	○	○	○	○	○	○	○
Meditate	○	○	○	○	○	○	○
Daily journaling	○	○	○	○	○	○	○
Exercise	○	○	○	○	○	○	○
Do something important	○	○	○	○	○	○	○
Do something good	○	○	○	○	○	○	○
Eat healthy	○	○	○	○	○	○	○
Read/listen to something good	○	○	○	○	○	○	○
Connect with others	○	○	○	○	○	○	○

WEEK OF:

MY PRIORITIES FOR THIS WEEK

GRATITUDE LOG:

MAIN GOALS:

DAILY ACTIVITIES

	M	T	W	T	F	S	S
Daily gratitude log	○	○	○	○	○	○	○
Do something fun	○	○	○	○	○	○	○
8 glasses of water	○	○	○	○	○	○	○
Meditate	○	○	○	○	○	○	○
Daily journaling	○	○	○	○	○	○	○
Exercise	○	○	○	○	○	○	○
Do something important	○	○	○	○	○	○	○
Do something good	○	○	○	○	○	○	○
Eat healthy	○	○	○	○	○	○	○
Read/listen to something good	○	○	○	○	○	○	○
Connect with others	○	○	○	○	○	○	○

MY PRIORITIES FOR THIS WEEK

GRATITUDE LOG:

MAIN GOALS:

DAILY ACTIVITIES

	M	T	W	T	F	S	S
Daily gratitude log	○	○	○	○	○	○	○
Do something fun	○	○	○	○	○	○	○
8 glasses of water	○	○	○	○	○	○	○
Meditate	○	○	○	○	○	○	○
Daily journaling	○	○	○	○	○	○	○
Exercise	○	○	○	○	○	○	○
Do something important	○	○	○	○	○	○	○
Do something good	○	○	○	○	○	○	○
Eat healthy	○	○	○	○	○	○	○
Read/listen to something good	○	○	○	○	○	○	○
Connect with others	○	○	○	○	○	○	○

WEEK OF:

MY PRIORITIES FOR THIS WEEK

GRATITUDE LOG:

MAIN GOALS:

DAILY ACTIVITIES

	M	T	W	T	F	S	S
Daily gratitude log	○	○	○	○	○	○	○
Do something fun	○	○	○	○	○	○	○
8 glasses of water	○	○	○	○	○	○	○
Meditate	○	○	○	○	○	○	○
Daily journaling	○	○	○	○	○	○	○
Exercise	○	○	○	○	○	○	○
Do something important	○	○	○	○	○	○	○
Do something good	○	○	○	○	○	○	○
Eat healthy	○	○	○	○	○	○	○
Read/listen to something good	○	○	○	○	○	○	○
Connect with others	○	○	○	○	○	○	○

MY PRIORITIES FOR THIS WEEK

GRATITUDE LOG:

MAIN GOALS:

DAILY ACTIVITIES

	M	T	W	T	F	S	S
Daily gratitude log	○	○	○	○	○	○	○
Do something fun	○	○	○	○	○	○	○
8 glasses of water	○	○	○	○	○	○	○
Meditate	○	○	○	○	○	○	○
Daily journaling	○	○	○	○	○	○	○
Exercise	○	○	○	○	○	○	○
Do something important	○	○	○	○	○	○	○
Do something good	○	○	○	○	○	○	○
Eat healthy	○	○	○	○	○	○	○
Read/listen to something good	○	○	○	○	○	○	○
Connect with others	○	○	○	○	○	○	○

WEEK OF:

MY PRIORITIES FOR THIS WEEK

GRATITUDE LOG:

MAIN GOALS:

DAILY ACTIVITIES

	M	T	W	T	F	S	S
Daily gratitude log	○	○	○	○	○	○	○
Do something fun	○	○	○	○	○	○	○
8 glasses of water	○	○	○	○	○	○	○
Meditate	○	○	○	○	○	○	○
Daily journaling	○	○	○	○	○	○	○
Exercise	○	○	○	○	○	○	○
Do something important	○	○	○	○	○	○	○
Do something good	○	○	○	○	○	○	○
Eat healthy	○	○	○	○	○	○	○
Read/listen to something good	○	○	○	○	○	○	○
Connect with others	○	○	○	○	○	○	○

live
your
dream.

Please can you help us? Leaving a review and rating on Amazon means others can discover and benefit from our wonderful books! Please leave a review :)

Only the truth of who you are, if realized, will set you free

Eckhart Tolle